For my grandfather, J. P. Williamson,
and my father, J. P. Williamson, Jr.

ACKNOWLEDGMENTS

Many thanks to J. P. Williamson, Jr., Doris Palmer, John Downing,
Antonia Felix, Cynthia Sternau, Anne and Tom Glisson, Ray Brooks,
Gerry Braun, Ulrich Brinkmann, Denise Bergstrom, Tom McCarthy,
Marie Drumm, Pat Barnett, Claudia Chadbourne, Fern Gorin, the Staff
at the Science and Technology Center of the New York Public Library,
and the community of St. Peter's Episopal Church in Chelsea.

designed and produced by
ons Limited

10116-0572
9-1241

und in Singapore

8-91-3

ine S. Williamson

rt M. Tod
or: Elizabeth Loonan
rt Director: Ron Pickless
rdinator: Heather Weigel
Edward Douglas
Cynthia Sternau
r: Shawna Kimber
hers: Julie Dewitt, Natalie Goldstein,
Cathy Stastny
ant: Laura Wyss
P: Blanc Verso/UK

PICTURE CREDITS

Art Resource/Alinari p. 9

Art Resource/Giraudon pp. 10-11, 13, 18

J. Allan Cash Ltd p. 31

Corbis-Bettmann pp. 7, 14 (bottom), 21 (top), 37, 47 (bottom), 48(top), 48 (bottom), 50, 52, 53, 56 (bottom), 60 (top), 65 (top)

Mary Evans Picture Library pp. 4, 6, 8, 12, 17, 19, 22 (bottom), 23, 26, 36, 38 (bottom), 39, 40, 41 (top), 44, 45, 46, 49, 51, 58, 59, 62, 66 (top), 67, 72, 73

William B. Folsom p. 76 (top)

Hulton Deutsch Collection Ltd pp. 15, 32 (top), 33 (bottom), 34 (top), 34 (bottom)

Mirror Syndication International pp. 5, 42, 57, 60 (bottom), 61, 64 (top), 64 (bottom), 66 (bottom)

New York Public Library pp. 16, 25, 65 (bottom)

Chris Taylor/Sylvia Cordaiy Photo Library Ltd p. 24

Topham Picture Source pp. 20 (top), 20 (bottom), 21 (bottom), 22 (top), 27, 28, 29, 30, 32 (bottom), 33 (top), 38 (top), 41 (bottom), 42 (top), 43, 47 (top), 54, 55, 56 (top), 63, 70 (top), 70 (bottom), 74 (top), 74 (bottom), 75, 77, 78

UPI/Corbis-Bettman p. 69, 71

Wright Brothers National Memorial Museum p. 14 (top)

The
GOLDEN A
of
AVIATI

KATHERINE S. WILI

TODTRI

This book wa
Todtri Produc
P.O. Box 572
New York, N
FAX: (212) 2

Printed and b

ISBN 1-88090

Author: Kathe

Publisher: Rol
Editorial Dire
Designer and
Production Co
Senior Editor:
Project Editor
Associate Edit
Picture Resear
    Kate Lewi
Research Assis

Typeset and D